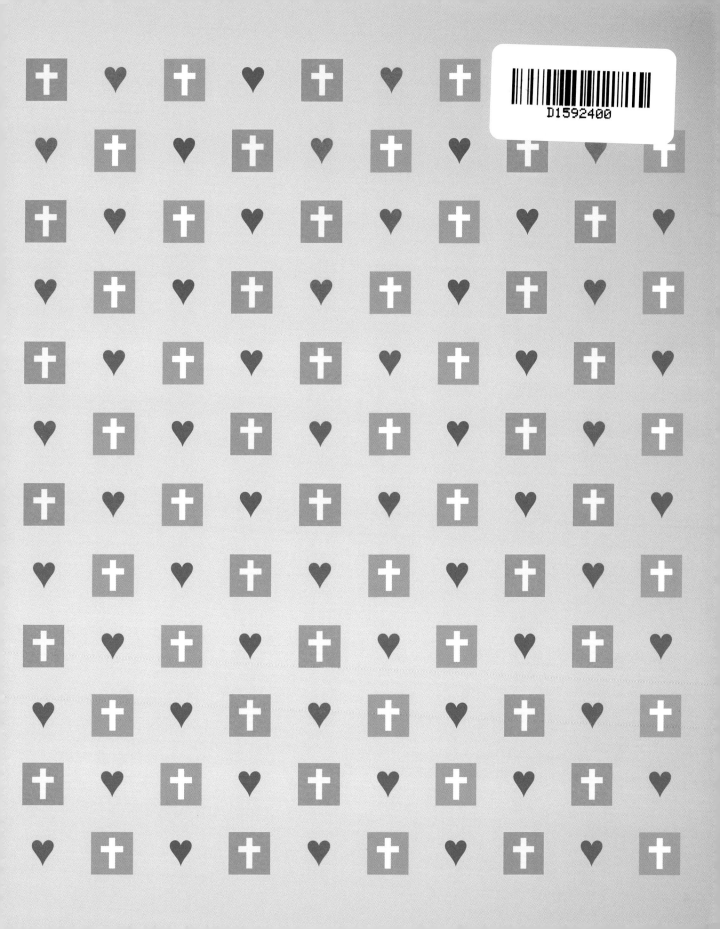

This book belongs to

_____

First edition 2023
This edition published 2023 by
Ascension Publishing Group, LLC.

Copyright © 2023 Anno Domini Publishing
www.ad-publishing.co.uk
Text copyright © 2023 Suzy Senior
Illustrations copyright © 2023 Dubravka Kolanovic

Publishing Director: Annette Reynolds
Designer: Jacqui Crawford
Pre-production: Kev Holt, GingerPromo

Editorial review for Ascension by Amy Welborn.

Ascension
PO Box 1990
West Chester, PA 19380
www.ascensionpress.com
1-800-376-0520

ISBN 978-1-954881-98-3

Printed in the United States of America
23 24 25 26 27 5 4 3 2 1

BASED ON THE PARABLE OF THE LOST SHEEP

Not There, Little Bear!

Written by
Suzy Senior

Illustrated by
Dubravka Kolanovic

ASCENSION
Kids

West Chester, PA

Little Bear peeked into the caterpillar house and smiled. Everybody looked happy.

4

Tickle and Nibbles were munching a leaf.
Wriggle was taking a walk on the walls,
and Stretchy was doing some gymnastics.
Most of the others were fast asleep—
rolled into balls or stretched out
peacefully on their twigs.

Little Bear began to count them. He loved his caterpillar friends and liked to make sure they were all safe before he went off to play.

It took a LONG while, but finally, "... 95, 96," he counted, peering under every leaf and twig, "97, 98, 99 ...

Oh!" he gasped.

"There should be 100!

ROVER IS MISSING!"

"Rover, where ARE you?" worried Little Bear. He left the others safely in their house and went off to search.

He checked behind the storybooks and under the desk. No, not there!

He looked in the fruit bowl and
even inside his dad's hat.
No, not there!

"**W**hat **ARE** you doing?" sighed his big sister. "You're always fussing over those caterpillars. Why don't you just leave it? You've still got **LOADS** of others!"

"NO!"

cried Little Bear.

"Rover is special. Actually, they're ALL special. Just because there are lots of them, doesn't mean they're not important!"

His sister just laughed and shook her head, but Little Bear kept searching.

"**R**over, where **ARE** you?"
He checked all around the backyard.
No, not there!

He paddled soggily
along the stream.
No, not there!

He poked his nose
into Woodpecker's cellar.
No, not there, either!

He nearly got his paw stuck
in Mole's doorway!

But no. Absolutely, definitely, NOT THERE!

Little Bear kept searching, all morning and right through lunchtime.

"Rover, where ARE you?"

14

He picked through mossy logs and crispy leaves.

He peered through tufty vegetable patches and drying laundry.

He was **DETERMINED** to find her!

15

By now Little Bear's tummy was growling hungrily—
and he felt SO tired. He wished everything was back to
normal and he could snuggle up on the sofa and rest.

Then he had a thought ...

THE SOFA!

17

As fast as his little paws would take him,
he hurtled back past the vegetable patch …

Past the logs and leaves …

Past Mole …

Past Woodpecker …

Past the stream …

And straight into the den …

...Just as his sister was about to sit down on the sofa!

"STOP!"

he yelled.

Puffing, he raced over and carefully
moved the cushions.

And there—
wiggling fearlessly
along the seat—was …

"ROVER!"

"THERE you are!"

"Oh, Rover!" cried Little Bear, lifting her to safety. "I'm SO glad I've found you!"

"And I'M glad you found her too," admitted his sister.

"That was a close one!"

Gently, Little Bear placed Rover back inside
her house.
He watched her wriggle off to meet the others,
and he smiled.

At long last, he plopped down onto the sofa. But guess what—NOW he didn't feel like resting! He was just TOO happy! He bounced up and down with joy. He made up a little song and sang it at the top of his voice!

And before long, **EVERYBODY** knew just how
happy Little Bear was to have Rover back home.

NOW THE TAX COLLECTORS and sinners were all drawing near to hear him. And the Pharisees and the scribes murmured, saying, "This man receives sinners and eats with them." So he told them this parable: "What man of you, having a hundred sheep, if he has lost one of them, does not leave the ninety-nine in the wilderness, and go after the one which is lost, until he finds it? And when he has found it, he lays it on his shoulders, rejoicing.

And when he comes home, he calls together his friends and his neighbors, saying to them, 'Rejoice with me, for I have found my sheep which was lost.' Just so, I tell you, there will be more joy in heaven over one sinner who repents than over ninety-nine righteous persons who need no repentance."

–Luke 15:1–7

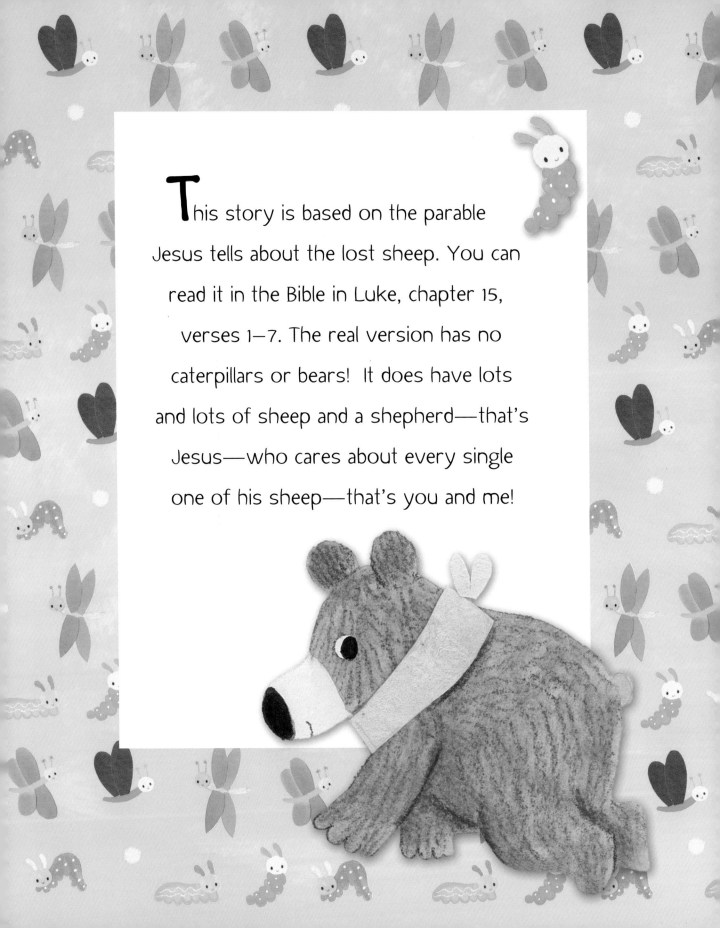

This story is based on the parable Jesus tells about the lost sheep. You can read it in the Bible in Luke, chapter 15, verses 1—7. The real version has no caterpillars or bears! It does have lots and lots of sheep and a shepherd—that's Jesus—who cares about every single one of his sheep—that's you and me!